Forest Biome

by Grace Hansen

Abdo
BIOMES
Kids

abdopublishing.com

Published by Abdo Kids, a division of ABDO, PO Box 398166, Minneapolis, Minnesota 55439.

Printed in the United States of America, North Mankato, Minnesota.

052016

092016

 THIS BOOK CONTAINS RECYCLED MATERIALS

Photo Credits: iStock, Shutterstock

Production Contributors: Teddy Borth, Jennie Forsberg, Grace Hansen

Design Contributors: Laura Mitchell, Dorothy Toth

Cataloging-in-Publication Data

Names: Hansen, Grace, author.

Title: Forest biome / by Grace Hansen.

Description: Minneapolis, MN : Abdo Kids, [2017] | Series: Biomes |
    Includes bibliographical references and index.

Identifiers: LCCN 2015959102 | ISBN 9781680805017 (lib. bdg.) |
    ISBN 9781680805574 (ebook) | ISBN 9781680806137 (Read-to-me ebook)

Subjects: LCSH: Forest ecology--Juvenile literature.

Classification: DDC 577.3--dc23

LC record available at http://lccn.loc.gov/2015959102

Table of Contents

What is a Biome?

A biome is a large area. It has certain plants and animals. It also has a certain climate.

desert

forest

freshwater

marine

grassland

tundra

5

Forest Biomes

There are three main forest biomes. Temperate forests are found in temperate regions. These forests experience four seasons. Leaves fall off the trees in autumn.

7

Boreal forests are in high northern **latitudes**. They have two main seasons. Summers are short and warm. Winters are long and cold. Snow is the main form of **precipitation**.

Tropical forests are near the **equator**. The two main seasons are rainy and dry. Both are very hot.

11

Plants

Temperate forests have lots of different plants. They have oak, elm, maple, and many other trees. Ferns, wildflowers, and mosses grow, too.

Boreal forests have **evergreen** trees. Evergreens have leaves called needles. Pine, fir, and spruce trees are evergreens.

15

Tropical forests have lots of plants. They have orchids and mosses. Over 100 tree species grow in tropical forests.

17

Animals

Forests are homes to many animals. Moose, wolves, and bears live in boreal forests. Wolves and bears also live in temperate forests. Kangaroos and tigers live in them, too!

Many animals live in tropical forests. Green iguanas live in these forests. Orangutans and sloths live in them, too.

Things You Might See in a Forest Biome

boreal

caribou moss

lynx

temperate

aspen tree

white-tailed deer

tropical

lianas

tamarin monkey

Glossary

climate – weather conditions that are usual in an area over a long period of time.

equator – an imaginary line drawn around the Earth that divides it into the northern and southern hemispheres.

evergreen – a plant that keeps its green leaves throughout the year.

latitude – distance north or south of the equator.

precipitation – water that falls to the ground.

Index

abdokids.com

Use this code to log on to abdokids.com and access crafts, games, videos, and more!

Abdo Kids Code:
BFK5017